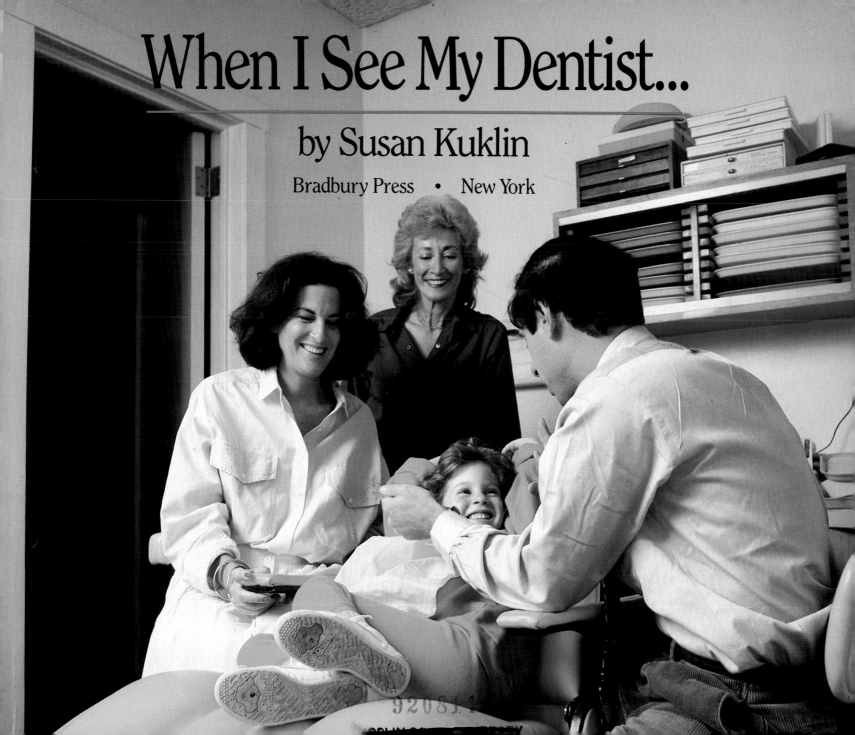

When I See My Dentist...

by Susan Kuklin

Bradbury Press • New York

The author wishes to thank

Erica Wolff

Judith Wolff

Dr. Steven Grossman

Marcia Paley

First Presbyterian Church Nursery School

Marjorie Goldsmith

Flora Bryant

Denise Jeffers

Dr. Joel Goldin

Dr. Amy Bona

Dr. Marc Patenaude

Sharon Steinhoff

Lynn Braswell

Bradbury Press
An Affiliate of Macmillan, Inc.
866 Third Avenue, New York, N.Y. 10022
Collier Macmillan Canada, Inc.
Printed and bound in the United States of America

10 9 8 7 6 5 4 3 2 1

Library of Congress Cataloging-in-Publication Data

Kuklin, Susan.

When I see my dentist.

Summary: Four-year-old Erica describes her visit to
the dentist for a checkup.
1. Dentistry—Juvenile literature.   2. Children—
Preparation for dental care—Juvenile literature.
[1. Dentistry.   2. Dental care]   I. Title.
RK63.K85   1988   617.6′01   87-25695
ISBN 0-02-751231-2

for Bailey

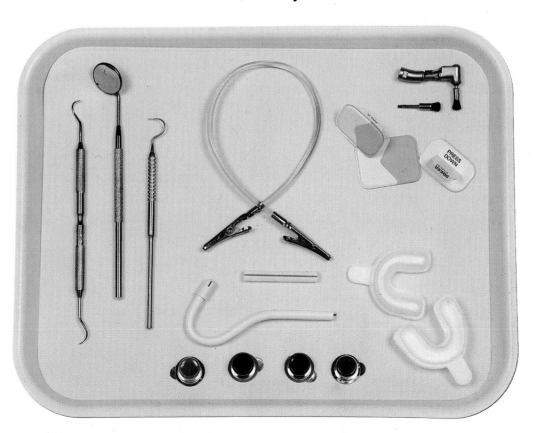

The first time I saw my dentist I was two and a half. My baby teeth were all grown in, so I was ready for a checkup. Now, every six months, my dentist examines my teeth to make sure they are strong and healthy.

At this visit I'm four years old, and I already know how easy it's going to be.

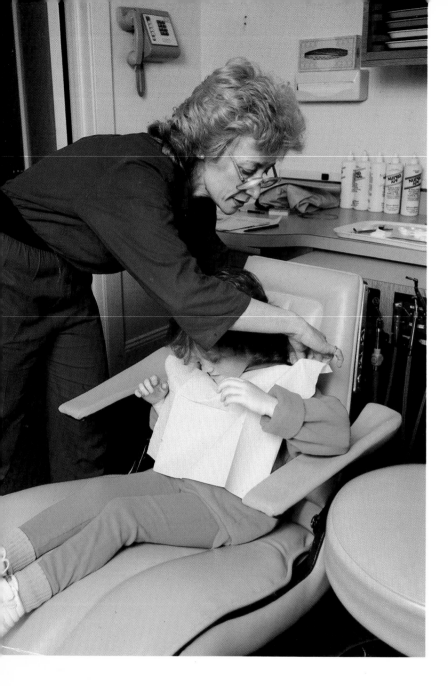

When my name is called, I climb into a large yellow chair in the dentist's office. Marcia, the dentist's assistant, washes her hands. Then she puts a large paper bib on me.

"This will keep your beautiful outfit clean, Erica," she says, as she adjusts my chair. "Are you comfortable now?"

I nod yes and Marcia goes on. She asks me when I brush and if I know why sugar is bad for my teeth. I tell her I brush at night and in the morning, but I don't know about sugar.

Marcia explains, "Sugar is food to some germs that live in our mouths. Soon after the germs eat it, they make acid. This acid forms the holes in our teeth that we call cavities."

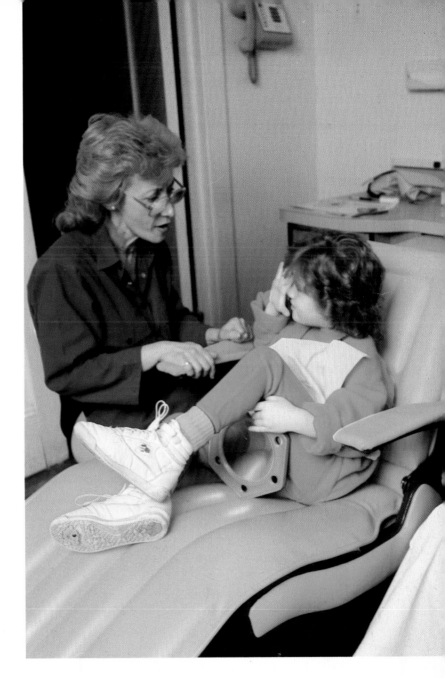

INSTRUMENT: large mirror

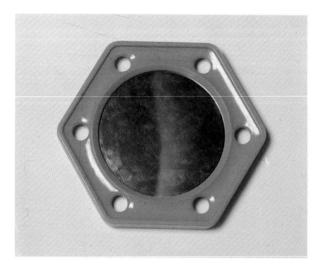

Marcia wants to see how many baby teeth I have. She gives me a mirror so that I can watch as she counts.

I have ten teeth on the top and ten on the bottom. "Twenty primary teeth," Marcia says. "That's the right number."

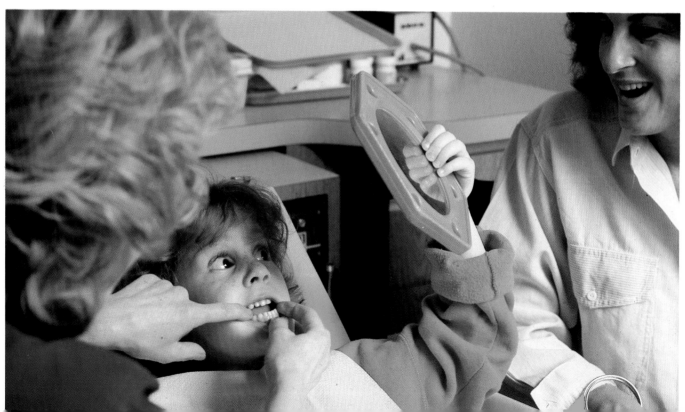

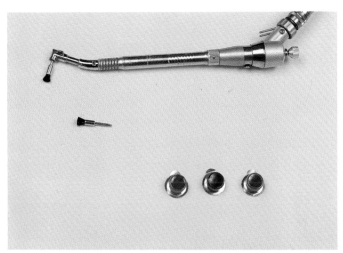

The dentist's toothbrush is on a long cord. Marcia pulls it out, turns it on, and lets me touch the tip. It's soft and tickles my finger.

I get to choose the toothpaste flavor. Cherry.

"Open as big as you can...a little bigger, bigger...," says Marcia. She cleans one tooth at a time. I like the way it makes my mouth feel.

INSTRUMENT: water spray and saliva ejectors

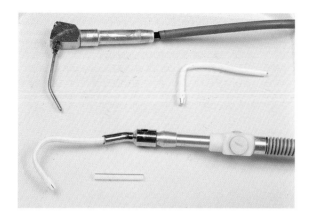

Sometimes Marcia squirts a little water in my mouth to rinse out the toothpaste. My mouth is also wet with saliva, which my friend Thomas calls spit.

Marcia puts a red and white straw into my mouth to suck out all the water. "This is a saliva ejector," she explains.

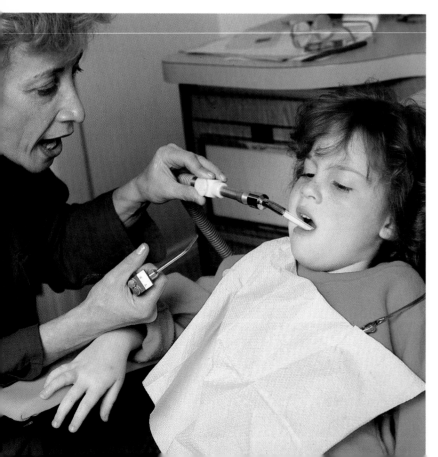

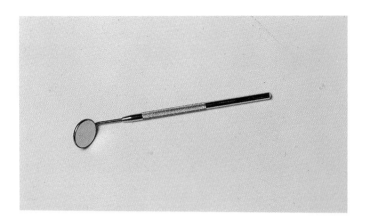

Now my teeth feel clean. I watch as Marcia uses a tiny mirror to check her work. I can see a little bit of brown on the back of my teeth.

Marcia tells me, "Food, germs, and saliva make a kind of brown stain."

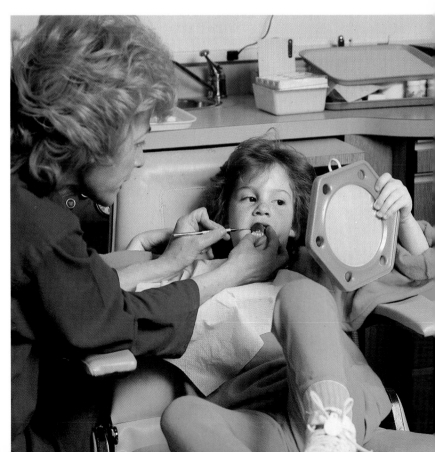

INSTRUMENT: scaler

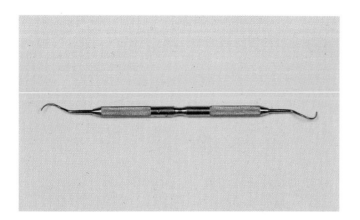

To get it off, Marcia takes out an instrument called a scaler. She puts the curved part of the scaler on my fingernail to show me how it scrapes away the stain. It feels like a gentle tickle, a gentle scratch. Then she cleans the brown from my teeth.

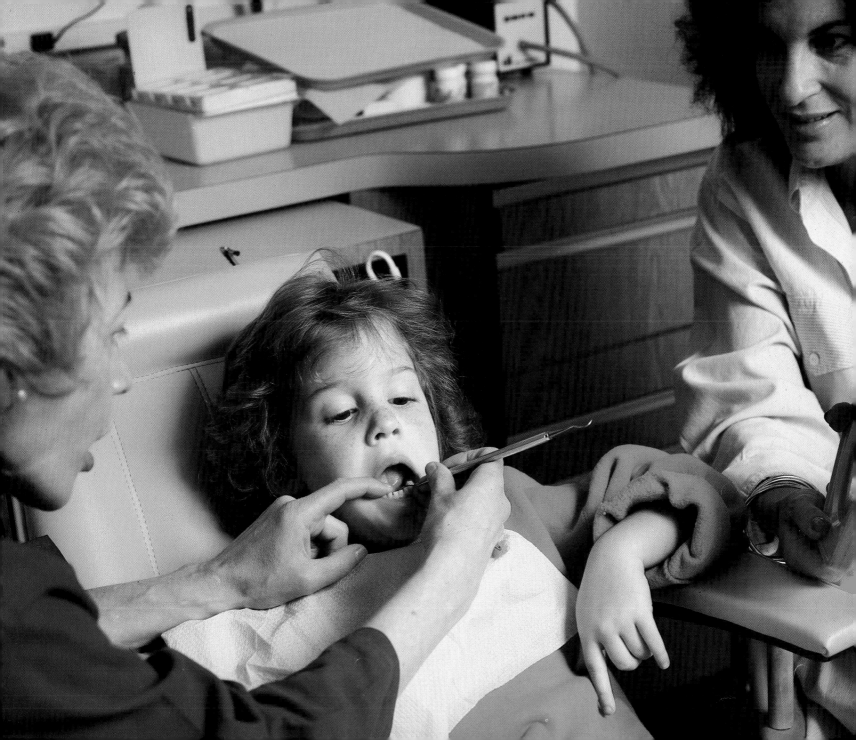

INSTRUMENT AND TREATMENT: fluoride with holders and saliva ejectors

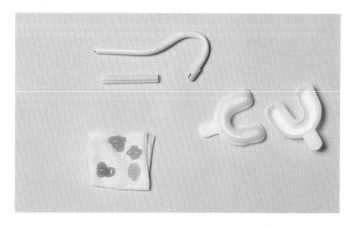

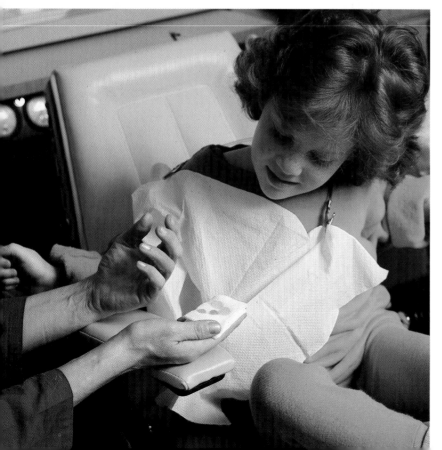

Next Marcia brings out the fluoride. I get it at every six-month visit. The fluoride comes in lots of different flavors—apple, mint, bubble gum, and cherry. I choose bubble gum. Fluoride makes my teeth strong and protects them from acid.

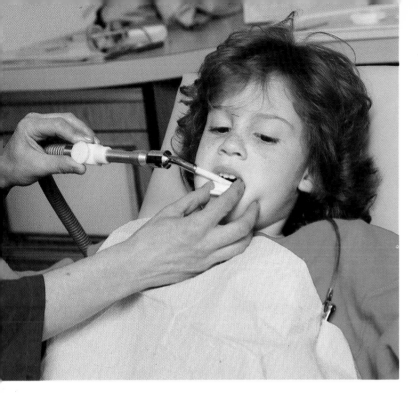

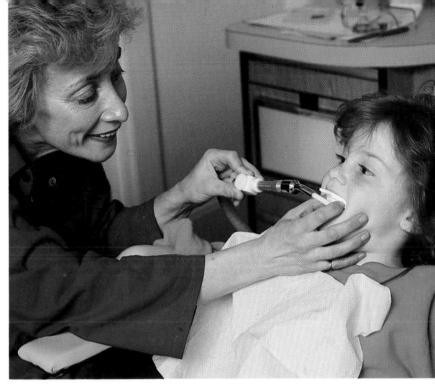

Marcia places a holder filled with fluoride over my bottom teeth. It feels soft. She keeps it there for four minutes while she tells me stories. So my mouth stays dry, she uses the saliva ejector. Then she puts the fluoride on the top teeth in the same way. I get a "Fluoride at Work" sticker when she's done.

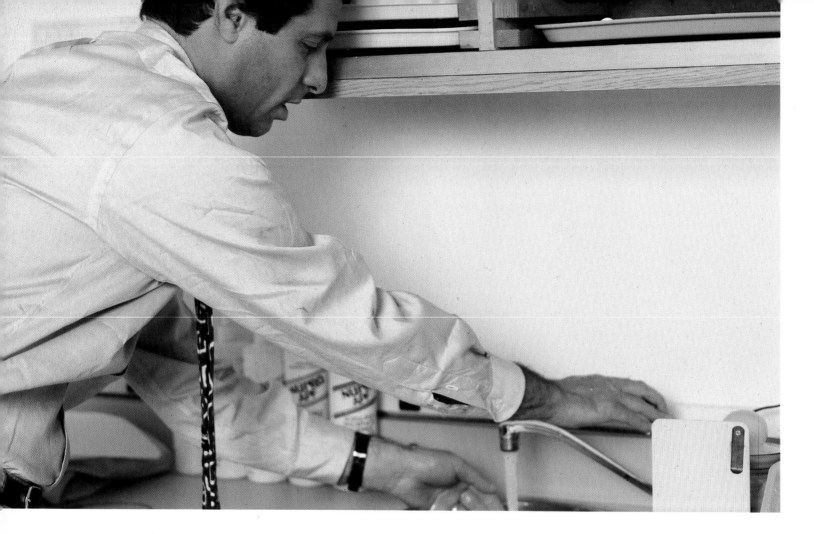

At last, Dr. Steve comes into the room and washes his hands. They must be clean when he touches my mouth.

"How often are you brushing your teeth?" he asks. When I tell him that I do it every night and every morning, he gives me a big smile and says, "That's terrific."

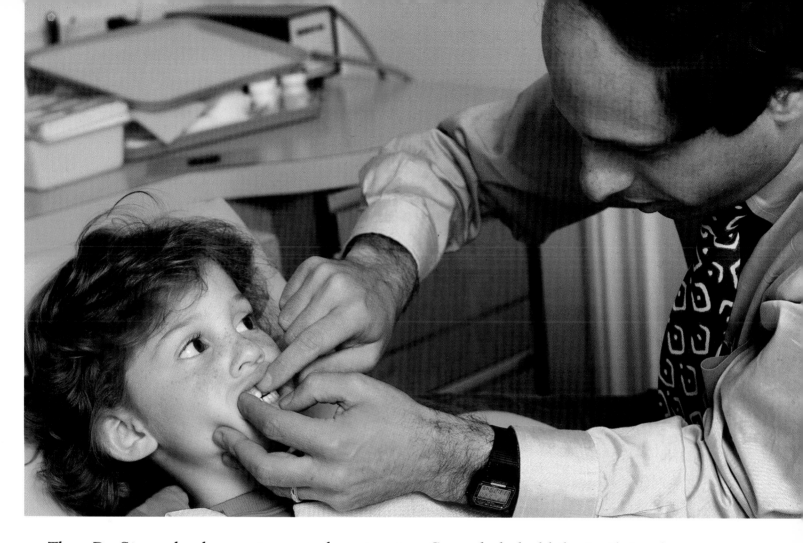

Then Dr. Steve checks my gums and my tongue. Gums help hold the teeth in place. And tongues are not just for talking. When we eat, they move food on and off the teeth.

Dr. Steve tells me, "Wonderful, Erica, no bumps, no swelling, and no sores."

INSTRUMENT: explorer

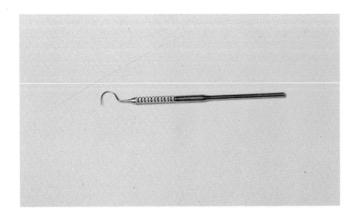

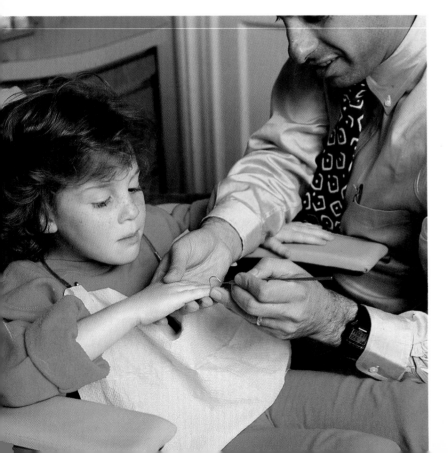

He first looks closely at all my teeth with his little mirror. Then he takes up an instrument called an explorer. On my fingernail, Dr. Steve shows me how he's going to use it to count and closely examine my teeth. I feel it lightly tap, tap, tap.

"Now we're ready," Dr. Steve says, reaching for his mirror. "Open wide, Erica. I can't stand on my head."

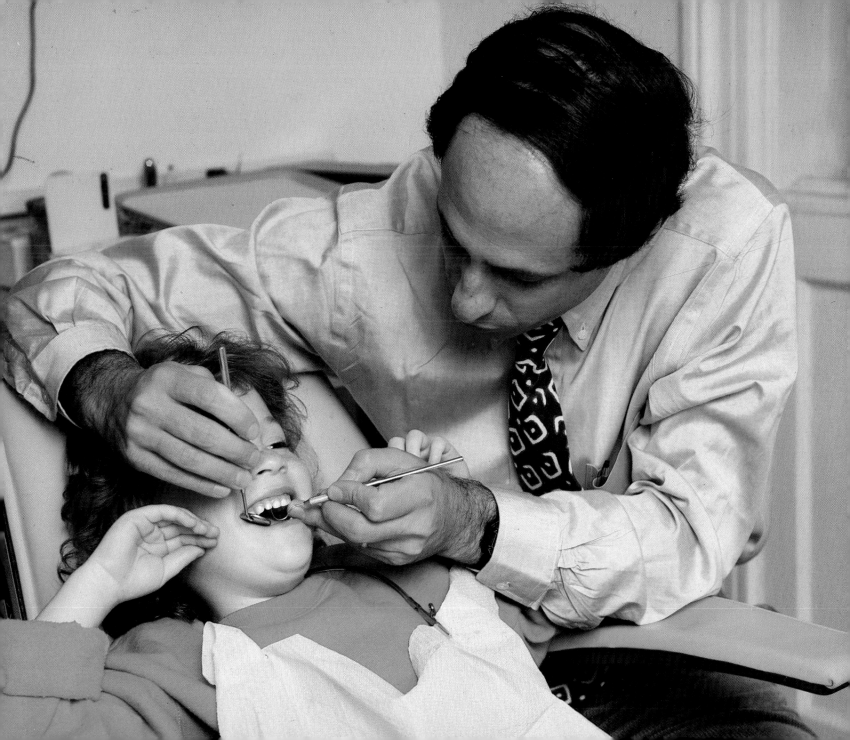

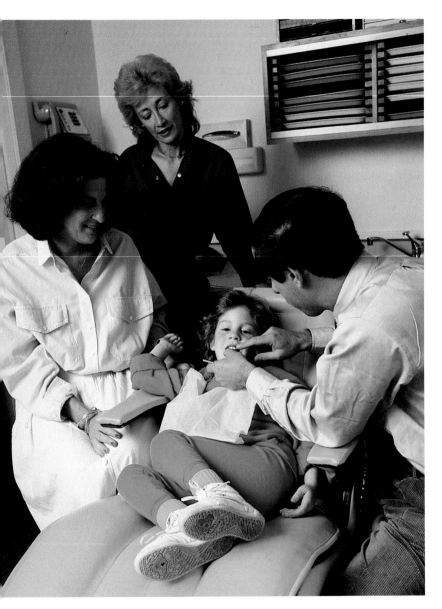

Next Dr. Steve holds my lips and asks me to bite down. He explains that this will help him check the outside of my teeth. While Mommy watches I open, shut, open, shut.

"Everything looks good," Dr. Steve says. "Your jaw moves beautifully, and your teeth fit together just right."

Then the bib comes off and I start to go.

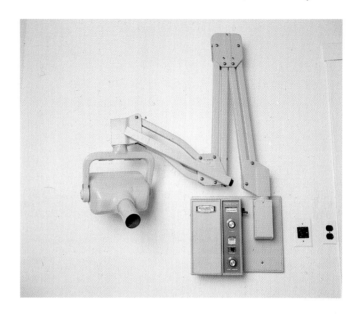

"Wait," Dr. Steve says. "I need to take pictures of your upper and lower teeth to see how they're growing and to double-check for cavities.

"I'm going to use a special kind of camera that uses X-rays to take pictures." He points to the machine on the wall next to me.

"I can't put the film in that big camera, so I will put it inside your mouth." He shows me a little package of paper that holds the X-ray film.

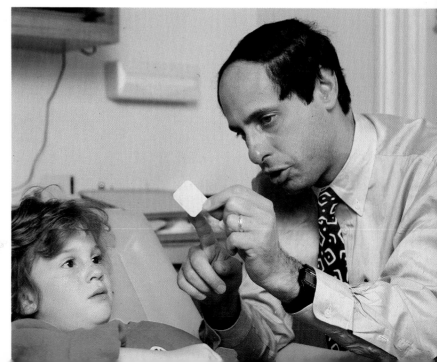

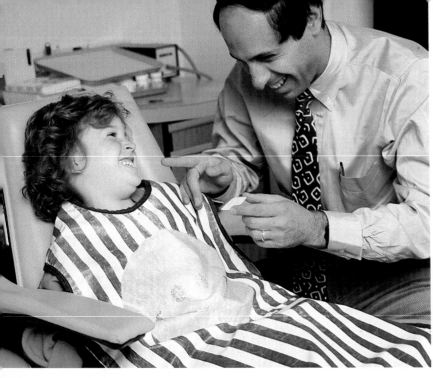

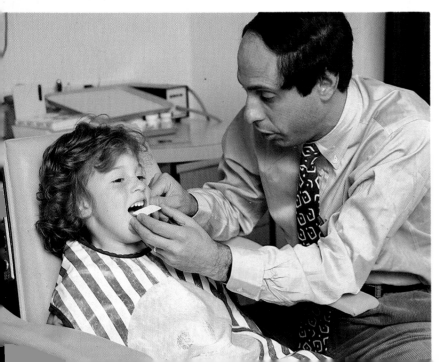

For these pictures Marcia takes off my bib and puts a heavy apron on me. It is made of metal, but it is soft. My dentist explains, "The reason you're going to wear this is because we don't want the X-rays on the rest of you."

Dr. Steve places a package of film in my mouth. "Now bite very softly, not hard." To X-ray my upper teeth, he puts the camera's nose right by my nose.

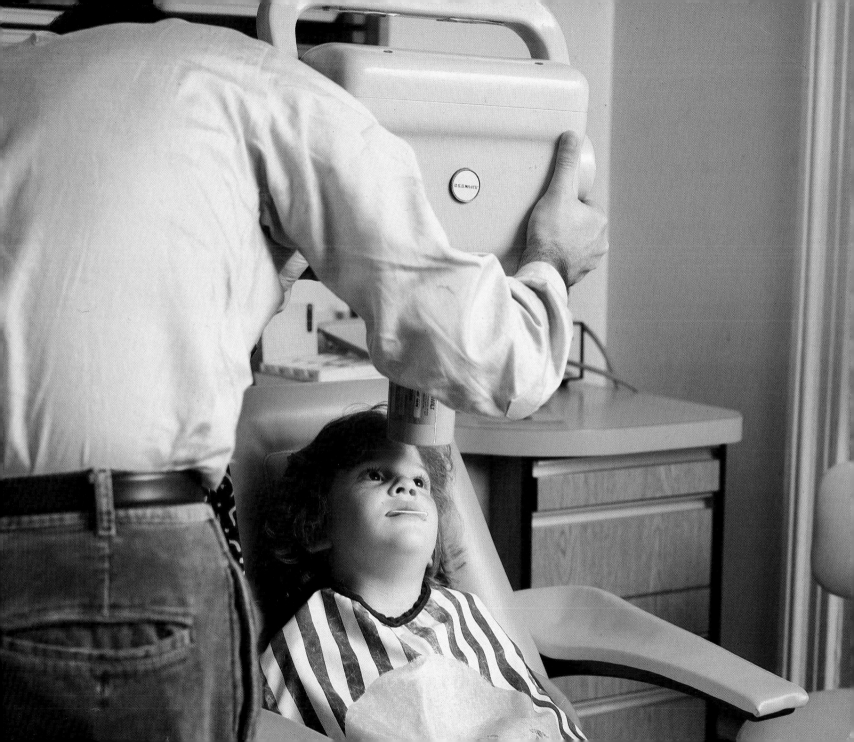

I have to keep my head straight and still. Dr. Steve walks out of the room to press a button. The camera goes *beep*. I don't feel a thing. For my lower teeth, he moves the camera's nose to my chin and puts another package of film in my mouth. *Beep*.

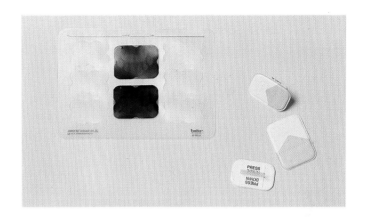

X-ray film, package, and Erica's X-rays

After a few minutes Dr. Steve returns. "Want to see some beautiful teeth?" he asks. He shows me my very own X-rays. Then Marcia gives me another sticker! This one says, "No cavities."

Dr. Steve goes on. "Now you've got to keep up the good work, Erica. Soon your permanent teeth will come in. As they grow, your baby teeth will loosen and fall out. In the back of your mouth you will get new teeth called molars. They have lots of hills and valleys. You will have all your permanent teeth forever, so make sure you keep them clean."

Now Marcia shows me big make-believe teeth and a huge toothbrush. "Let's go over how to brush your teeth correctly, Erica," she says.

She places the big brush where the gums meet the teeth. Then she moves it sideways with a back and forth motion.

Marcia cleans all over. "Don't forget to brush the inside part of the teeth, even the ones way in the back," she reminds me.

"I won't," I tell her, laughing. "I'll brush mine till they look just like those."

When Dr. Steve returns with a balloon, I know it's time to go. "Your teeth are perfect, Erica," he says. "We'll see you in six months."

I'm sorry to have to wave good-bye so soon. Then Mommy tells me she has a checkup with her dentist next week. "Don't worry, Mommy," I say, "going to the dentist is quick and easy and fun."

HOW I WROTE THIS BOOK

Like its companion, *When I See My Doctor . . .* , this book had its roots at the First Presbyterian Church Nursery School in New York City. At the school's invitation, I led a discussion about the students' experiences at the dentist. I was impressed by how eager and enthusiastic the children were about their visits. Erica Wolff was no exception.

Erica's dentist, Dr. Steven Grossman, gave me permission to photograph and tape record Erica's actual examination. I interviewed him before the checkup in order to learn how he handled specific procedures in pediatric dentistry. Some of these procedures may differ from dentist to dentist, such as having the child be accompanied by a parent or care-giver, but in general the scene depicted in this book is what most children experience.

By the time Erica arrived for her examination, my assistant and I had set up my Dyna-Lite M-1000 power pack strobe with one head and photographed all the dentist's instruments. My camera was a Hasselblad 500C/M with a 100mm lens and a 50mm lens. A Leica M-4 camera with a 35mm lens was my backup. All the film was Kodachrome 64.

As the book progressed, I made return trips to the class so the children could see how a book is made. Special thanks to Erica's teacher, Flora Bryant, her assistant, Denise Jeffers, student aide Doria Meyers, and Erica's classmates: Heather Cleary, Alexander Eames, Austin Fremont, Kristin Gialella, Thomas Gilliland, Andrew Halpern, Charles Hurd, Kushal Karan, Jason Loos, Ying Yue Li, Nora Kelleher, Kurtlan Massarsky, Alexandra Moss, Nicholas Movshon, Emma Smith-Stevens, Elizabeth Thaler, and Abby Vladeck.